weird but true!

OCEAN

NATIONAL
GEOGRAPHIC
KiDS

weird but true!

OCEAN

300
FIN-TASTIC FACTS FROM
THE DEEP BLUE SEA

NATIONAL GEOGRAPHIC
WASHINGTON, D.C.

Whale sharks' skin can be up to **four inches** (10 cm) **thick.**

4

A kid could easily **fit inside** a whale shark's mouth.

Octopuses have a **doughnut-shaped brain.**

Damselfish "weed" the algae they don't like from algae gardens.

Octopus ink **CONFUSES** a predator's senses of **TASTE** and **SMELL.**

MORE THAN 50 SHIPS HAVE DISAPPEARED IN AN AREA OF THE NORTH ATLANTIC OCEAN BETWEEN FLORIDA, BERMUDA, AND PUERTO RICO.

The area is called the BERMUDA TRIANGLE, or the DEVIL'S TRIANGLE.

GIANT TUBE WORMS THAT LIVE NEAR UNDERSEA HYDROTHERMAL VENTS CAN BE TALLER THAN THE AVERAGE NBA BASKETBALL PLAYER.

DIANA NYAD SWAM NONSTOP FOR NEARLY 53 HOURS FROM CUBA TO KEY WEST, FLORIDA, U.S.A.—A DISTANCE OF

110 MILES
(177 KM).

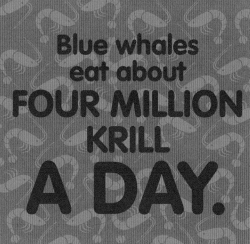

Blue whales eat about **FOUR MILLION KRILL A DAY.**

The Hawaiian word* for **monk seal** translates to **"dog running in rough seas."**

*The word is *ilio holo i ka uaua.*

SCIENTISTS THINK THAT OCEAN WATER 3.5 BILLION YEARS AGO WAS AS MUCH AS TWO TIMES SALTIER THAN TODAY'S OCEAN WATER.

Some chitons—small MOLLUSKS living in tide pools—have hundreds of tiny "EYES" in their hard shells that SENSE LIGHT AND DARK.

PUFFINS HAVE **BACKWARD-FACING** SPINES ON THE ROOF OF THEIR MOUTH THAT HELP KEEP CAPTURED **FISH FROM ESCAPING.**

YUM!

The world's tallest mountain, Mauna Kea, in Hawaii, U.S.A., **rises 32,696 feet** (9,966 m), but **most of it is underwater.**

Walruses **squirt water** at sand on the ocean floor to **uncover** buried mollusks.

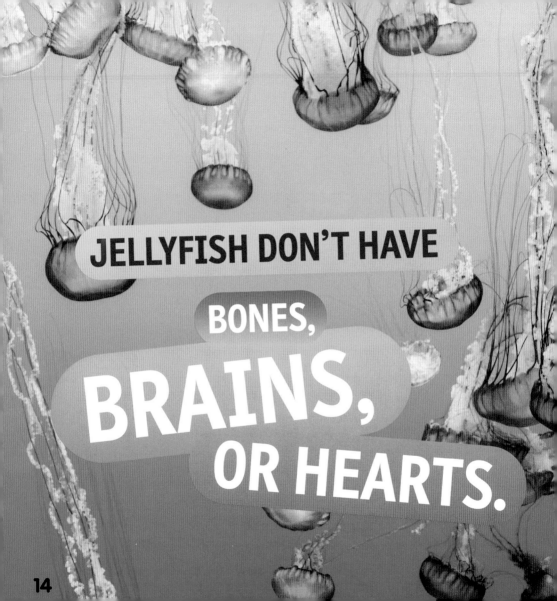

JELLYFISH DON'T HAVE BONES, **BRAINS,** OR HEARTS.

14

It was said that the **KRAKEN**, the **SEA MONSTER** of Nordic myth, attracted fish by **SPREADING ITS POOP** on the water's surface.

DIVERS DISCOVERED PREHISTORIC PAINTINGS AND ENGRAVINGS IN A CAVE IN FRANCE 121 FEET (37 M) UNDERWATER.

16

Humpback whales make "NETS" OF BUBBLES to herd fish into a tight group for easier gulping.

17

Dumbo octopuses get their name because their "fins" resemble **the ears** of the cartoon **elephant.**

The insides of sockeye salmon turn **ORANGE** from the krill they eat.

CORAL SKELETONS AND **HUMAN BONES** HAVE SIMILAR STRUCTURES.

Sunflower sea stars are born with **five arms** but can **grow up to 24 arms** by adulthood.

THE LION'S MANE NUDIBRANCH, A SEA SLUG, MAKES A SECRETION THAT SMELLS LIKE WATERMELON.

Green bomber worms release tiny balloon structures that burst into **glowing light** to distract predators.

Flying fish can launch themselves out of the water and glide the length of about seven basketball courts.

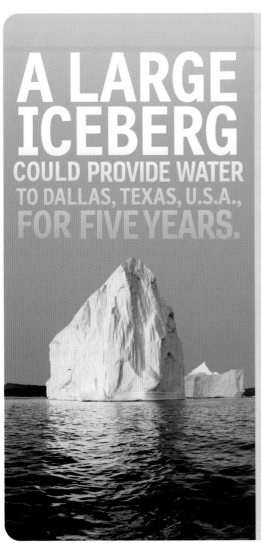

A LARGE ICEBERG
COULD PROVIDE WATER TO DALLAS, TEXAS, U.S.A., FOR FIVE YEARS.

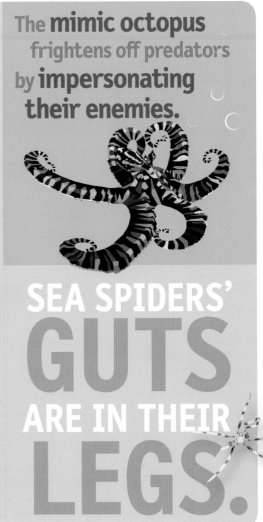

The **mimic octopus** frightens off predators by **impersonating** their enemies.

SEA SPIDERS' GUTS ARE IN THEIR LEGS.

23

To reduce noise,

the columns and rails of the **Kraken** roller coaster in Orlando, Florida, U.S.A., are filled with sand.

The world's largest cruise ship has **20 restaurants,** **an ice rink,** and **a zip line.**

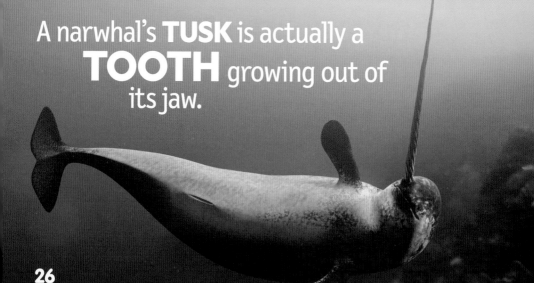

A narwhal's **TUSK** is actually a **TOOTH** growing out of its jaw.

Scientists think a **SALTY OCEAN** lies under the **ICY SURFACE** of Europa, one of Jupiter's moons.

Many of the Bajau people of Southeast Asia are able to **free-dive** underwater for **three minutes or more.**

IT'S ESTIMATED THAT THERE'S ENOUGH **SALT** IN THE OCEAN TO **BURY THE CONTINENTS 500 FEET (150 M) DEEP.**

You can do it!

JELLYFISH swam in oceans **BEFORE DINOSAURS** roamed Earth.

IN ARGENTINA, ORCAS SOMETIMES THROW THEMSELVES ONSHORE TO CATCH SEA LIONS.

Scientists discovered a 240-million-year-old fossil of a 16-foot (5-m)-long ichthyosaur* with a 13-foot (4-m)-long thalattosaur* in its belly.

*Marine reptile

COLOSSAL SQUID HAVE **HOOKS** AND **TEETH** ON THEIR SUCKERS, HELPING THEM **GRAB** AND **HOLD** ON TO **PREY.**

PACIFIC OCEAN

OCEANIC POLE OF INACCESSIBILITY
× 48°52.6'S 123°23.6'W
(POINT NEMO)

SOUTHERN OCEAN

Tahiti

Ducie Island

Chile

Maher Island

POINT NEMO, located in the Pacific Ocean, is **CLOSER** to the **INTERNATIONAL SPACE STATION** than to the **NEAREST LANDMASS.**

Check out my pearly purples!

A horn shark's **TEETH** are sometimes stained **PURPLE** after eating sea urchins.

A 1,000-pound (450-kg) manatee can **EAT 100 POUNDS (45 KG) OF PLANTS** in 24 hours.

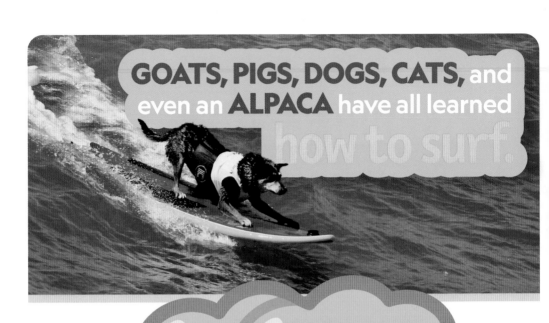

GOATS, PIGS, DOGS, CATS, and even an **ALPACA** have all learned how to surf.

A sperm whale has the **largest brain** of any animal—it weighs **five times more** than a human's.

34

Blooms of tiny plankton in the ocean can be seen from space.

In 1947, the Norwegian explorer Thor Heyerdahl and his crew sailed across some **4,300 MILES (6,920 km)** of the Pacific Ocean in a **RAFT MADE ONLY OF BALSA WOOD.**

Goblin sharks have
EXTENDABLE
JAWS
that they use
to snatch prey.

Sea stars use seawater instead of blood to pump nutrients through their bodies.

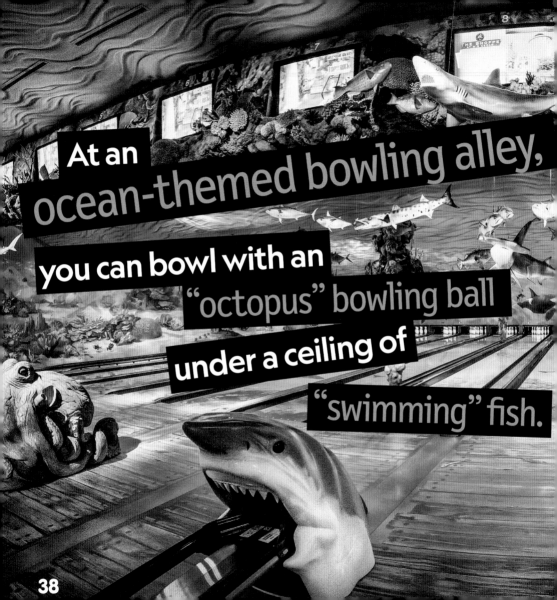

At an ocean-themed bowling alley, you can bowl with an "octopus" bowling ball under a ceiling of "swimming" fish.

SOME SPECIES OF ALBATROSS CAN **FLY AROUND THE GLOBE** IN JUST OVER A MONTH.

Sand dollars use small, fuzzy **spines** to move along the sand underwater.

40

To escape predators, penguins can JUMP up to 10 feet (3 m) from the water onto ice.

Just before jumping, they RELEASE AIR BUBBLES from their feathers, which helps them move faster.

One company used jellyfish proteins to make ice cream that **GLOWED** when you licked it.

Some scientists think that life on Earth began in the **ocean.**

The **GIANT PACIFIC OCTOPUS,** which can grow to be 20 feet (6 m) wide, is the size of a **GRAIN OF RICE** when it's hatched.

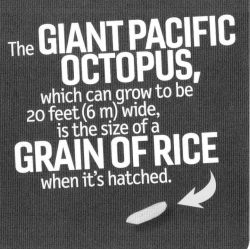

Manta rays regularly visit coral reefs so that fish will nibble parasites off their skin.

Crown-of-thorns sea stars eat by **EXTRUDING THEIR STOMACH** out of their mouth to cover their prey.

They can go for **NINE MONTHS** without a meal.

The **MYTHOLOGICAL CREATURE** known as the asp-turtle was said to be **SO LARGE** that sailors **DOCKED ON IT** thinking that it was an island, but then were pulled under the sea.

Hop on... if you dare!

The first **COLOR UNDERWATER PHOTOGRAPH,** taken in 1926, was of a **HOGFISH.**

THE AMOUNT OF **KRILL** LIVING AROUND ANTARCTICA WEIGHS MORE THAN **500** MILLION LARGE **BENGAL TIGERS.**

Sea pens got their name because they look like quill pens.

In ancient Greece, dentists used **STINGRAY VENOM** to numb their patients.

GIANT KELP SEAWEED **CAN GROW** **TWO FEET** (61 CM) **A DAY.**

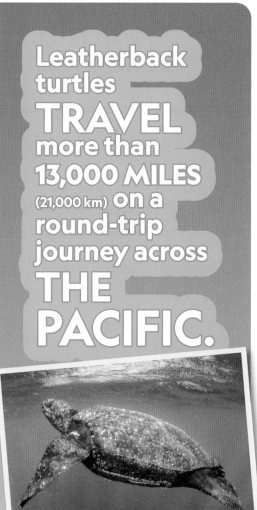

Leatherback turtles **TRAVEL** more than **13,000 MILES** (21,000 km) on a round-trip journey across **THE PACIFIC.**

A group of **BARRACUDA** is called a **BATTERY.**

A group of **STINGRAYS** is called a **FEVER.**

VAMPIRE SQUID DON'T SUCK BLOOD, BUT THEY DO EAT DEAD PLANKTON.

Sea cucumbers **BREATHE** through their REAR END.

Spotted dolphins

are born without spots.

Weddell seals make **loud calls underwater** that can be heard from the icy surface **above.**

Scientists found a 2,000-YEAR-OLD DEVICE used to calculate the movement of the SUN, MOON, AND PLANETS in a shipwreck in the Mediterranean Sea.

COASTAL MANGROVE FORESTS HAVE TANGLED, STILT-LIKE ROOTS THAT CAN WITHSTAND **daily flooding** FROM HIGH TIDES.

Australia's Great Barrier Reef has some 3,000 CORAL REEFS and 600 INDIVIDUAL ISLANDS.

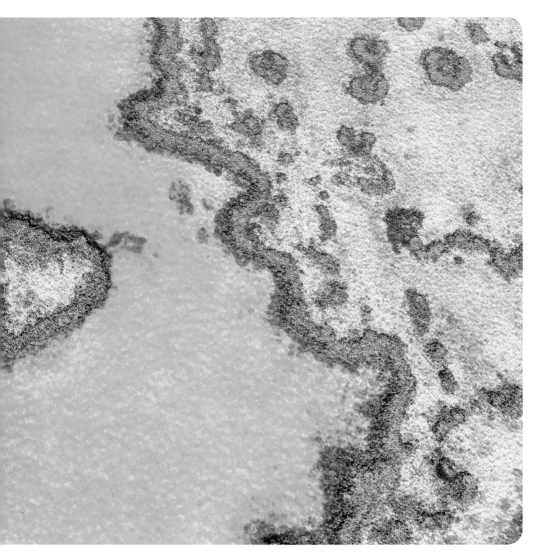

More than **90 PERCENT** of the world's trade travels in **CARGO SHIPS** on the ocean.

Shortfin makos, the **FASTEST** sharks in the ocean, are also known as blue dynamites.

The long-spined sea urchin has **POISONOUS,** foot-long (30-cm) spines.

THE UGLY ANIMAL PRESERVATION SOCIETY ONCE NAMED THE BLOBFISH THE WORLD'S UGLIEST FISH.

Rude.

Some sharks are **COLOR-BLIND.**

Off the coast of Dubai, **300** ARTIFICIAL ISLANDS were designed to resemble a world map when viewed from above.

The bowhead whale uses its GIGANTIC HEAD to break through ice.

Earth's largest known waterfall lies **underwater** between Greenland and Iceland.

A TEENAGE GIRL HAS COLLECTED MORE THAN **50,000 GOLF BALLS** HIT INTO THE OCEAN OFF THE COAST OF CENTRAL CALIFORNIA, U.S.A.

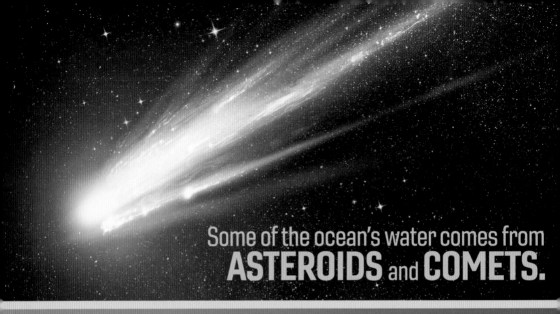

Some of the ocean's water comes from
ASTEROIDS and **COMETS.**

Feather stars,
relatives of sea stars,
catch their prey with
**STICKY,
VELCRO-LIKE
TUBE FEET.**

THE RED HANDFISH HAS A SET OF FINS THAT LOOK LIKE HUMAN HANDS.

Diners at Subsix Restaurant in the Maldives eat dinner 20 feet (6 m) **UNDER THE INDIAN OCEAN.**

Deep-sea-dwelling vampire squid can squirt colorless ink that **twinkles** with bioluminescent light.

Octopuses in aquariums can **open closed containers** to get to the food inside.

An erupting **UNDERSEA VOLCANO** in the South Pacific created a **FLOATING ISLAND OF PUMICE** that was more than **40 TIMES** the size of **CENTRAL PARK** in New York City.

Coral reefs exist on **less than one percent** of the ocean floor.

I'm deadly cute!

ONE **PUFFERFISH** CONTAINS ENOUGH **POISON** TO KILL **30 ADULTS.**

Sand mason worms live in a protective **tube** **that they build** with shell fragments and sand.

Despite the nickname "SEA COW," manatees are more closely related to elephants.

All clownfish are **born male,** but some switch to female later.

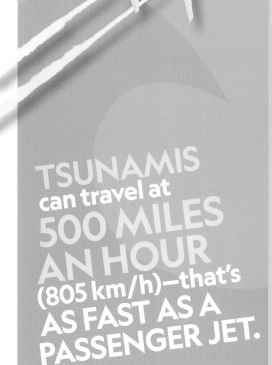

TSUNAMIS can travel at **500 MILES AN HOUR** (805 km/h)—that's AS FAST AS A PASSENGER JET.

The surface of the Pacific Ocean is **larger** than the land area of all the continents **combined.**

WHEN FLEEING PREDATORS, GREEN SEA TURTLES CAN SWIM AS FAST AS THE FASTEST MAN ON EARTH CAN RUN.

In medieval Europe, cups made from **narwhal tusks** were thought to **protect** the drinker **from being poisoned.**

Deep-sea bamboo corals can be **taller** than a **three-story building.**

THE CRUSHING PRESSURE OF THE WATER IN THE MARIANA TRENCH EQUALS THAT OF 50 **JUMBO JETS** PILED ON A PERSON.

Seaweed can have **more** protein

than **chicken** does.

SOME PIRATE SHIPS HAD FULL-TIME BANDS TO PLAY SEA SHANTIES.

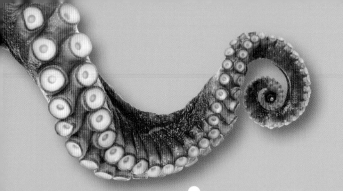

The **giant** Pacific octopus has more than

2,000 suction cups on its body.

Octopuses **taste** with their **suction cups.**

Cabezons will EAT ABALONES* and then SPIT OUT their shells.

*A type of mollusk

Penguins pant to stay cool, just like dogs do.

The energy in a hurricane's clouds and rain could produce about 200 times the amount of electricity needed to power the entire world.

75

Sea lice are **DARKER** during the day to protect themselves from the **SUN'S RAYS.**

MARIANA SNAILFISH HAVE GAPS IN THEIR SKULL THAT HELP THEM WITHSTAND THE PRESSURE OF THE **DEEPEST PART OF THE OCEAN.**

THE TITANIC HAD ITS OWN DAILY NEWSPAPER.

Orcas sometimes work together to make waves that tip penguins and sea lions off ice floes.

The olive sea snake can **go for TWO HOURS** WITHOUT having to **take a BREATH OF AIR.**

SOME TYPES OF OYSTERS CLOSE THEIR SHELLS MORE WHEN THE MOON IS FULL. THEY OPEN THEM WIDER DURING NEW MOONS.

When a molting Humboldt penguin lost all its feathers in just one day, zookeepers fitted it with a wet suit to keep it from getting a sunburn.

IN WORLD WAR II, DUTCH SAILORS DISGUISED A WARSHIP AS A FLOATING ISLAND TO AVOID ENEMY DETECTION.

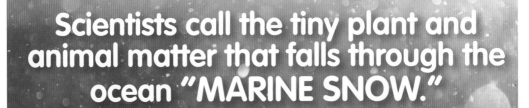

Scientists call the tiny plant and animal matter that falls through the ocean "MARINE SNOW."

Some flakes of marine snow can **FALL FOR WEEKS** before reaching the ocean floor.

SCIENTISTS SENT GUMMY BEARS TO THE **BOTTOM OF THE OCEAN** TO SHOW THE EFFECTS OF DEEP-SEA PRESSURE.

(The candy was crushed.)

Deep-sea-dwelling coffinfish have **INFLATABLE GILL CHAMBERS** that allow them to **HOLD THEIR BREATH** for up to four minutes.

Coffinfish have special fins for "walking" on the ocean floor.

Sea otters keep rocks—**WHICH THEY USE TO OPEN CLAMS—** in **LOOSE SKIN** under their arms.

83

Rogue waves, which can TOPPLE ships without warning, can be as tall as a 10-STORY BUILDING.

A BOX JELLYFISH HAS 24 EYES, GIVING IT A 360-DEGREE VIEW OF ITS SURROUNDINGS.

Hydrothermal vents on the ocean floor can spew bits of

gold and silver.

The elasmosaur, a marine reptile that lived more than 66 million years ago, had a manatee-like body, giraffe-like neck, and snake-like head.

In one day, scuba divers cleaned up more than 2,500 pounds (1,130 kg) of **trash** off the **ocean floor** near southern Florida, U.S.A.

Divers found a 45-pound (20-kg) **dumbbell,** more than 100 pounds (45 kg) of **fishing line, cell phones,** and a **sign from a pier.**

A BROWN PELICAN'S **BILL** CAN HOLD **THREE TIMES MORE FOOD THAN** ITS **STOMACH.**

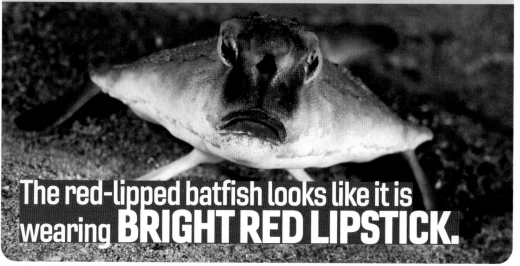

The red-lipped batfish looks like it is wearing **BRIGHT RED LIPSTICK.**

Engineers from Virginia, U.S.A., created a **jellyfish-like robot** that may one day be used for **underwater spy missions.**

Yeti crabs, found near hydrothermal vents in Antarctica, trap food in their **HAIRY ARMS.**

Scientists estimate that **less than 10 percent** of all ocean species have been **classified.**

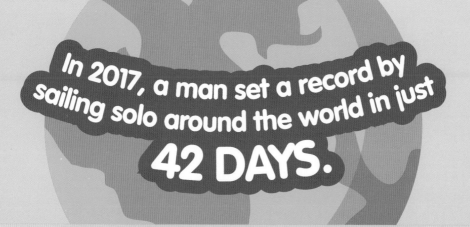

In 2017, a man set a record by sailing solo around the world in just **42 DAYS.**

Tire-size opahs, or **MOONFISH,** are the only known fully **WARM-BLOODED** fish.

In shallow water, corals

GLOW

pink and purple, which allows them to absorb sunlight and act as a sunscreen for the tiny plants that live inside them.

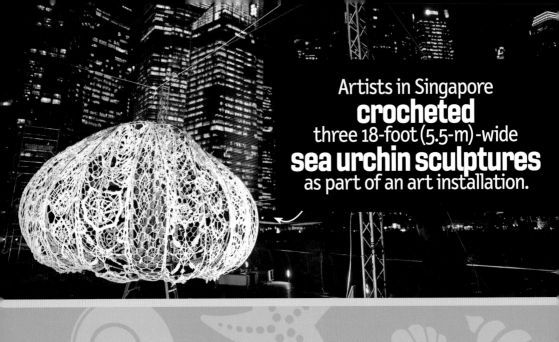

Artists in Singapore **crocheted** three 18-foot (5.5-m)-wide **sea urchin sculptures** as part of an art installation.

White-spotted pufferfish **build nests** on the ocean floor and decorate **them with shells.**

All aboard!

Remoras **hitch a ride** on sharks by attaching a **suction-cup-like disk** to a shark's skin.

93

The animators of *Finding Nemo* studied **dog faces** to create the **fishes' expressions.**

Seattle, Washington

New York New York

The 33 islands in the country of Kiribati STRETCH ACROSS 2,400 MILES (3,900 km)—

that's about the distance from NEW YORK CITY to SEATTLE, WASHINGTON STATE.

SEAHORSE COUPLES DANCE TOGETHER EVERY MORNING—SOMETIMES FOR HOURS.

THEY SOMETIMES ENTWINE TAILS SO THAT THEY DON'T LOSE EACH OTHER.

THE TRIO OF **MECHANICAL SHARKS** USED IN THE 1975 MOVIE *JAWS* WERE COLLECTIVELY NICKNAMED **BRUCE.**

Unicorn surgeonfish have spines on their tails that are as sharp as a scalpel.

Pacific warty octopuses are **wartier** the **deeper** they live in the ocean.

That's weird!

97

An artist has painted 100 murals of life-size whales and other sea life on the outside of buildings all over the world.

A swordfish produces an oil that covers its nose, repelling water and reducing drag.

WAVES AS TALL AS SKYSCRAPERS ROLL ALONG THE BOTTOM OF THE OCEAN THOUSANDS OF FEET BELOW THE SURFACE.

Horn sharks lay CORKSCREW-SHAPED eggs.

▶HORSESHOE CRABS **AREN'T CRABS—** THEY'RE RELATIVES OF SPIDERS.

▶ HORSESHOE CRABS HAVE **BLUE BLOOD.**

▶ THEY USE THEIR TAIL TO **FLIP THEMSELVES OVER** IF THEY GET STUCK ON THEIR BACK.

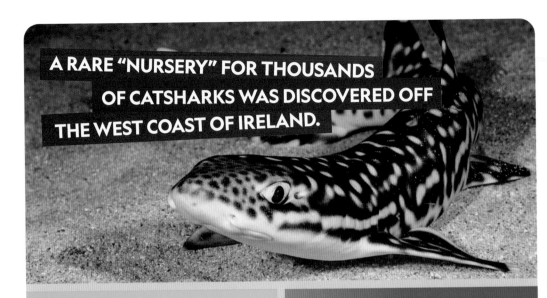

A RARE "NURSERY" FOR THOUSANDS OF CATSHARKS WAS DISCOVERED OFF THE WEST COAST OF IRELAND.

Cod have **taste buds** on a barbel beneath their chins.

A superstition holds that **whistling** on a warship can cause **dangerous winds.**

Ocean plants produce more than **half** of Earth's **oxygen.**

The ancient shark megalodon, which lived some 20 million years ago, was **LONGER THAN A SCHOOL BUS.**

The shark's jaws were so big that it could have **SWALLOWED A SMALL CAR.**

107

SAILORS HAVE SOMETIMES BEEN CALLED GOBS, HEARTIES, JACK-TARS, OR SEA DOGS.

Some 1,000 people live on a tiny island off the coast of Colombia, South America, that's the size of two soccer fields.

That's weird!

Early Europeans thought that every animal **on land** had a counterpart **in the sea—** like a sea mouse and a **sea rhino.**

109

There is enough
naturally
occurring
GOLD
**on the seafloor
to give each
person on Earth
NINE POUNDS
(4 kg) of it.**

There was
no ocean
**when Earth
first formed,
just molten
rock.**

**COOKIECUTTER
SHARKS** got their
name because they take
cookie-shaped
BITES
out of whales,
dolphins,
and fish.

VENUS FLYTRAP ANEMONES, WHICH RESEMBLE THEIR PLANT NAMESAKE, **GRAB AND STING** PREY WITH THEIR TENTACLES.

As a flatfish **GROWS,** one of its eyes **MOVES TO THE** **TOP** OF ITS HEAD.

Lobsters will EAT one another.

ONE BILLIONAIRE OWNS A
SUPER-YACHT THAT INCLUDES
A BASKETBALL COURT,
A MOVIE THEATER,
AND **ROOM FOR**
18 GUESTS.

Less than
5 PERCENT
of the ocean has
BEEN
EXPLORED.

PARROTFISH CAN **POOP OUT** HUNDREDS OF POUNDS OF SAND IN A YEAR.

PARROTFISH CAN **BITE THROUGH ROCK.**

That's weird!

HAWAII'S **WHITE-SAND BEACHES** ARE LARGELY MADE FROM PARROTFISH POOP.

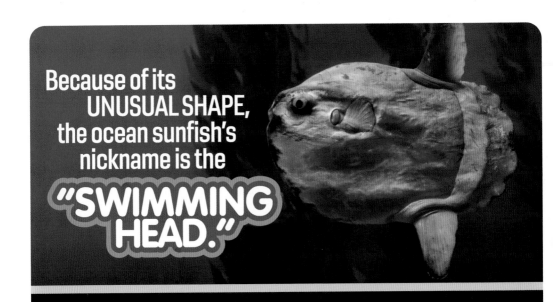

Because of its UNUSUAL SHAPE, the ocean sunfish's nickname is the **"SWIMMING HEAD."**

A small crustacean secretes a gel that acts like a **SUIT OF ARMOR,** protecting its body from the crushing deep-sea pressure.

STARGAZER FISH HAVE **EYES** ON TOP OF THEIR **HEADS.**

THEY BURY THEMSELVES IN SAND, WITH THEIR EYES POKING OUT, WAITING TO ATTACK PREY.

DAILY TIDES
IN THE
BAY OF FUNDY,

OFF THE COAST OF EASTERN CANADA, CAN RAISE THE WATER LEVEL MORE THAN
50 FEET.
(15 M)

Bowhead whales can live for more than

200
years.

A COLLECTION OF SEASHELLS WAS FOUND IN THE RUINS OF POMPEII.

A leafy sea dragon's fins provide camouflage so it blends into its seaweed-filled home.

Some **FOGBANKS** rolling in off the ocean look like **GIANT** tsunami waves.

Feeding cows **seaweed** makes them **burp less,** a recent study found.

A sea turtle can't pull its head into its shell.

EVERY YEAR, 705,000 TONS (640,000 T) OF "GHOST GEAR"—ABANDONED FISHING EQUIPMENT—IS LEFT IN THE OCEAN.

Giant clams can weigh more than a refrigerator.

Researchers fed great white sharks "BLUBBER BURRITOS"—seal blubber with sensors wrapped inside—to track their behaviors.

Fancy feet, eh?

MALE BLUE-FOOTED BOOBIES, A TYPE OF SEABIRD, SHOW OFF FOR FEMALES BY DOING A **HIGH-STEP STRUT.**

Scientists have found **REINDEER REMAINS** in the stomachs of Greenland sharks.

There are about **128 times** more islands in the Pacific Ocean than independent countries on Earth.

UNLIKE OTHER BEARS, POLAR BEARS HAVE **SMELLY FEET** THAT LEAVE **SCENT MARKS** ON THEIR ICY TERRAIN.

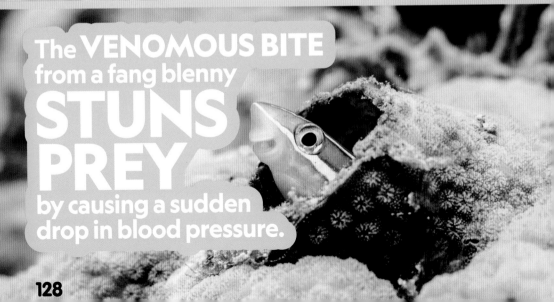

The **VENOMOUS BITE** from a fang blenny **STUNS PREY** by causing a sudden drop in blood pressure.

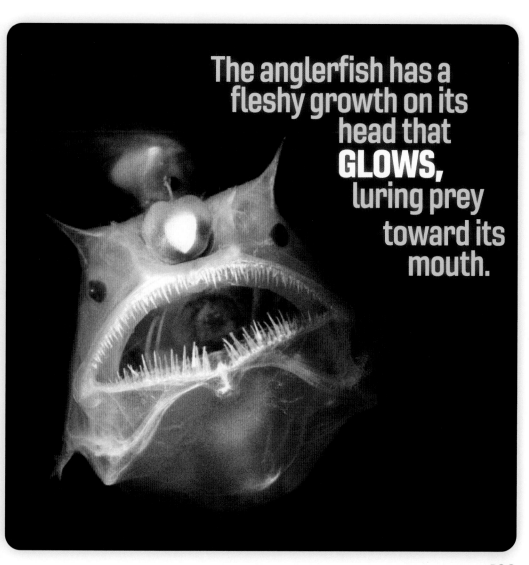

The anglerfish has a fleshy growth on its head that **GLOWS,** luring prey toward its mouth.

Brain coral got its name because it resembles a **human brain.**

A British artist made a **LIFE-SIZE DRAWING** of a 29.5-foot (9-m) giant squid using **squid ink.**

Seahorses can **move each of their eyes** independently.

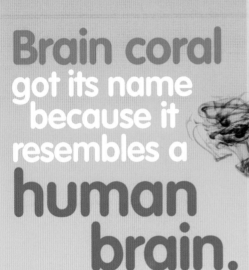

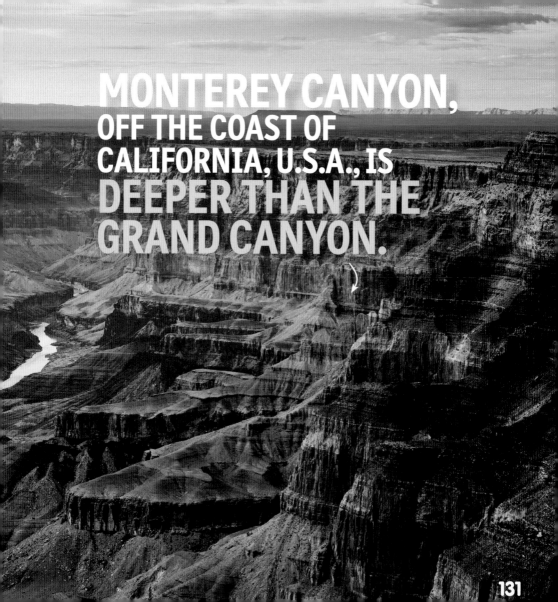

MONTEREY CANYON, OFF THE COAST OF CALIFORNIA, U.S.A., IS DEEPER THAN THE GRAND CANYON.

COLD WEATHER AND WIND IN FINLAND CAUSED

EGG-SHAPED
ICE BALLS
TO COVER A BEACH.

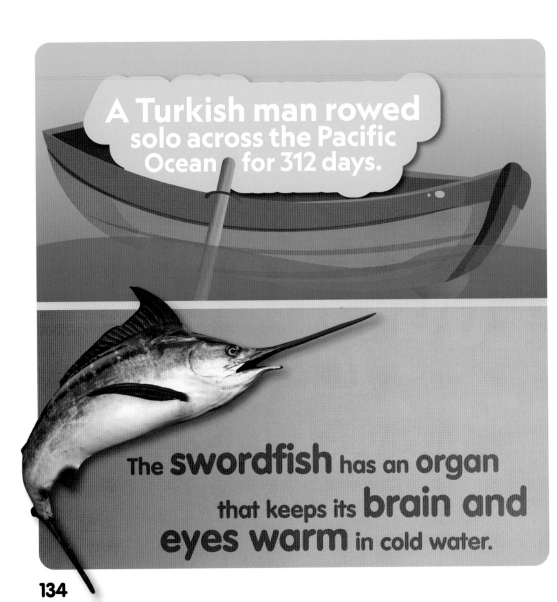

A Turkish man rowed solo across the Pacific Ocean for 312 days.

The **swordfish** has an **organ** that keeps its **brain and eyes warm** in cold water.

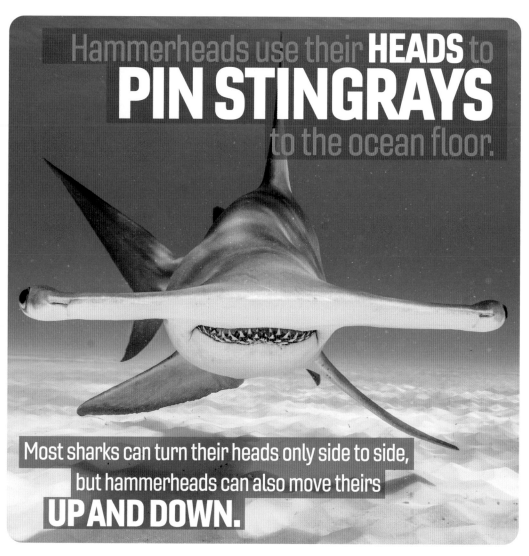

Hammerheads use their **HEADS** to **PIN STINGRAYS** to the ocean floor.

Most sharks can turn their heads only side to side, but hammerheads can also move theirs **UP AND DOWN.**

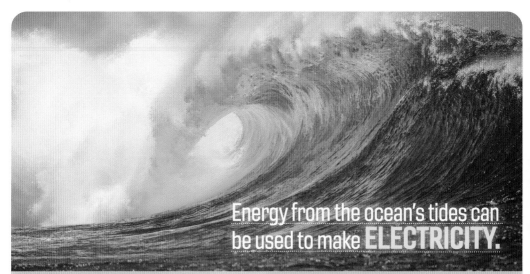

Energy from the ocean's tides can be used to make **ELECTRICITY.**

The prehistoric *Archelon* sea turtle was the **LENGTH OF A SMALL CAR.**

An animatronics designer created a remote-controlled "SPY OTTER" to give scientists an up-close look at sea otter life.

137

Deep-sea-dwelling **giant oarfish** can grow to be **longer than a school bus.**

The **KISSLIP CUTTLEFISH** gets its name from the **SMOOCH MARKS** on its body.

In Japanese folklore, a slender oarfish **washing ashore** signals that an **earthquake** may be **coming.**

THE PACIFIC OCEAN IS **FIVE TIMES WIDER** THAN THE MOON.

THE ORANGE-SPOTTED TUSKFISH OPENS CLAMS BY SMASHING THEM ON CORAL.

When opening a coconut, COCONUT CRABS produce more FORCE, pound for pound, than ANY OTHER ANIMAL ON EARTH.

Skeleton shrimp are sometimes called **"the praying mantises of the sea"** because of their **long bodies** and **legs.**

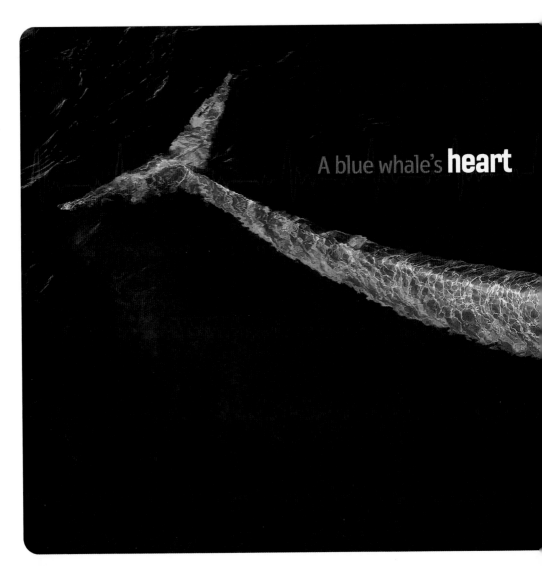

A blue whale's **heart**

beats only about **10 times** a minute.

(An adult human's heart beats 60 to 100 times a minute.)

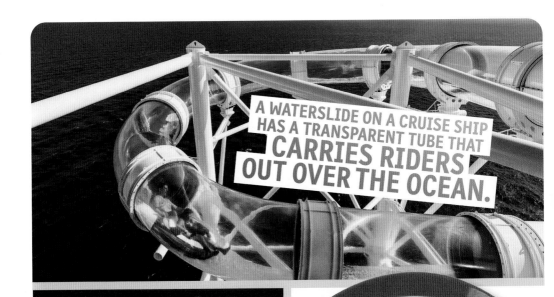

A WATERSLIDE ON A CRUISE SHIP HAS A TRANSPARENT TUBE THAT **CARRIES RIDERS OUT OVER THE OCEAN.**

A baby seahorse is called a **FRY.**

Giant squid have eyes the size of dinner plates.

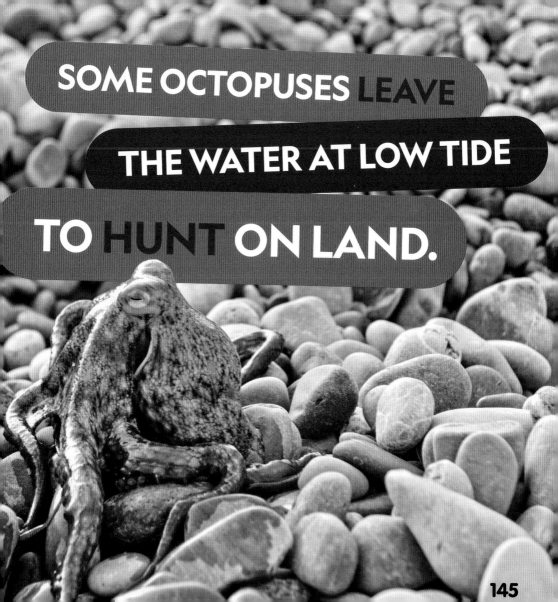

SOME OCTOPUSES LEAVE THE WATER AT LOW TIDE TO HUNT ON LAND.

When **seabirds** drink salt water, they secrete the **salt from** their **nostrils.**

Does anybody have a tissue?

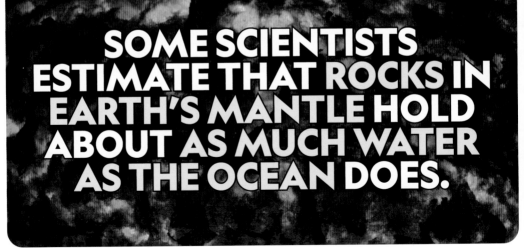

SOME SCIENTISTS ESTIMATE THAT ROCKS IN EARTH'S MANTLE HOLD ABOUT AS MUCH WATER AS THE OCEAN DOES.

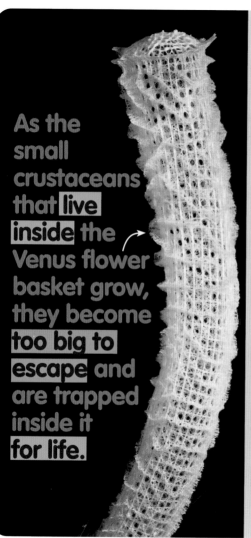

As the small crustaceans that **live inside** the Venus flower basket grow, they become **too big to escape** and are trapped inside it **for life.**

Hundreds of years ago, sailors in the Caribbean reported sighting **"MERMAIDS."**

(They were likely manatees.)

SAILFISH CAN FOLD DOWN THEIR LARGE DORSAL FIN TO MAKE THEM MORE STREAMLINED WHEN SWIMMING.

Sea otters were considered extinct until a rancher saw a small population off the California coast in 1938.

On the ice,
  penguins sometimes
"toboggan"
instead of walk—
      they lie on
  their stomach and
Wheeeee!
use their feet to
slide.

The NINJA LANTERNSHARK gets its name for its STEALTH AND JET-BLACK COLOR.

Some sea urchins produce a pigment that is used in a heart medicine.

Blue whale calves drink
100 gallons of milk
a day. (379 L)

They can gain eight pounds (4 kg)
every hour.

In 1979, oceanographer Sylvia Earle descended to the ocean floor strapped to the front of a submersible in an armored diving suit.

She walked on the ocean floor for two hours, setting a world record for the deepest untethered dive.

The **tentacles** of a lion's mane jellyfish

The Mid-Ocean Ridge—Earth's longest chain of mountains—is almost completely

underwater,

can stretch the length of a **blue whale.**

spanning more than 25 times the

length of the Himalaya.

The **CANDY CRAB** attaches coral polyps to its shell for **CAMOUFLAGE** in its coral home.

SPONGE CRABS camouflage themselves by attaching **SEA SPONGES** to their heads.

159

CALIFORNIA SEA HARES, A TYPE OF SEA SLUG, RELEASE **PURPLE INK** WHEN ATTACKED.

The Sri Lankan Navy rescued an **elephant** that got caught in a current and was **swept** into the **Indian Ocean.**

The deep-sea-dwelling **piglet squid** gets its name from its **pig-like shape.**

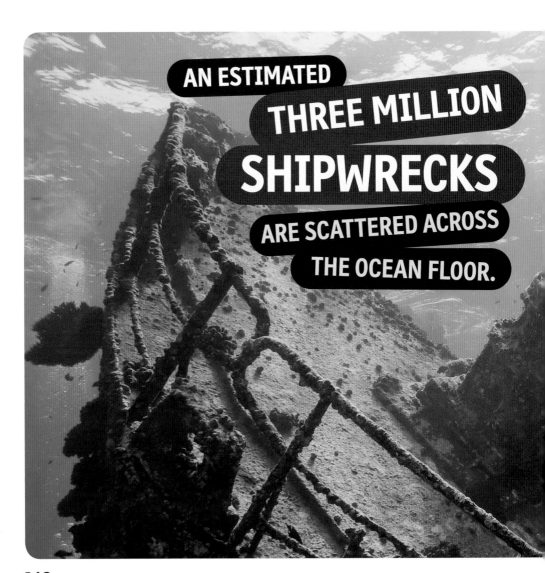

AN ESTIMATED **THREE MILLION** **SHIPWRECKS** ARE SCATTERED ACROSS THE OCEAN FLOOR.

SCIENTISTS BELIEVE MORE ARTIFACTS CAN BE FOUND IN SHIPWRECKS ON THE OCEAN FLOOR THAN IN ALL THE WORLD'S MUSEUMS COMBINED.

THE LONGHORN COWFISH HAS TWO PAIRS OF BULL-LIKE HORNS, WHICH MAKES IT HARD FOR MOST PREDATORS TO SWALLOW.

A BLUEFIN TUNA CAN **WEIGH** AS MUCH AS A **POLAR BEAR.**

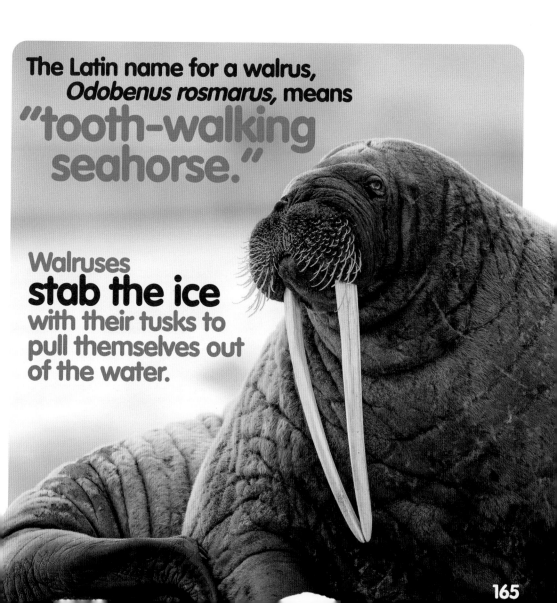

The Latin name for a walrus, *Odobenus rosmarus,* means "tooth-walking seahorse."

Walruses **stab the ice** with their tusks to pull themselves out of the water.

According
to legend, it's
bad luck
to change the
name of
a boat.

More people have
WALKED ON THE MOON than have
traveled to the
DEEPEST PART OF THE OCEAN,
Challenger Deep.

Great white sharks can
DETECT
a colony of seals located
TWO MILES (3.2 km) **AWAY.**

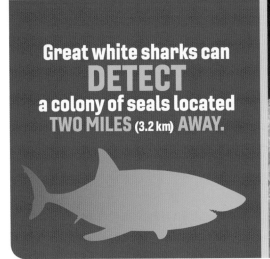

The goat that provided **MILK TO SAILORS** on two of Captain James Cook's voyages was **GIVEN A SILVER COLLAR** when she retired.

WHEN THREATENED, A SEA CUCUMBER EXPELS SOME OF ITS INTERNAL ORGANS TO DISTRACT PREDATORS—THEN GROWS THEM BACK LATER.

GIANT manta rays can grow **30 FEET** (9 m) across—

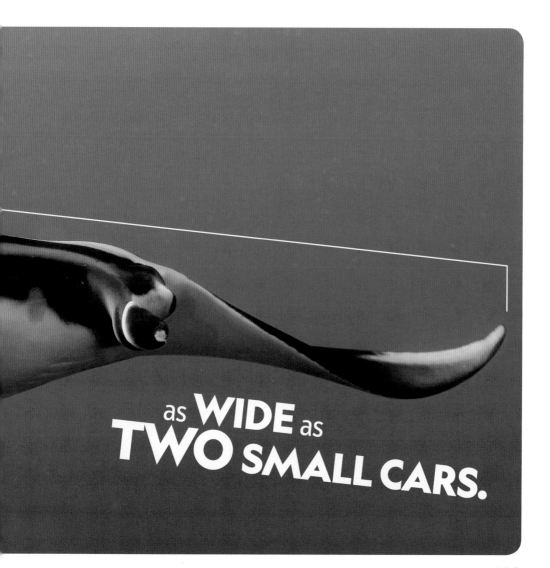

as **WIDE** as **TWO SMALL CARS.**

When attacking, great white sharks **ROLL BACK THEIR PUPILS,** making their eyes appear **white.**

YELLOW-BELLIED SEA SNAKES HYDRATE BY **DRINKING FRESH RAINWATER** THAT COLLECTS ON THE OCEAN'S SALTWATER SURFACE.

The largest dark spot on the moon is named the Ocean of Storms.

Sea turtles can stay **underwater** for **seven hours.**

In ancient Greek mythology, **Aphrodite,** **the goddess of love,** often was pictured with a **scallop shell.**

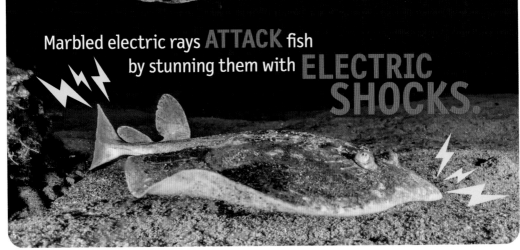

Marbled electric rays **ATTACK** fish by stunning them with **ELECTRIC SHOCKS.**

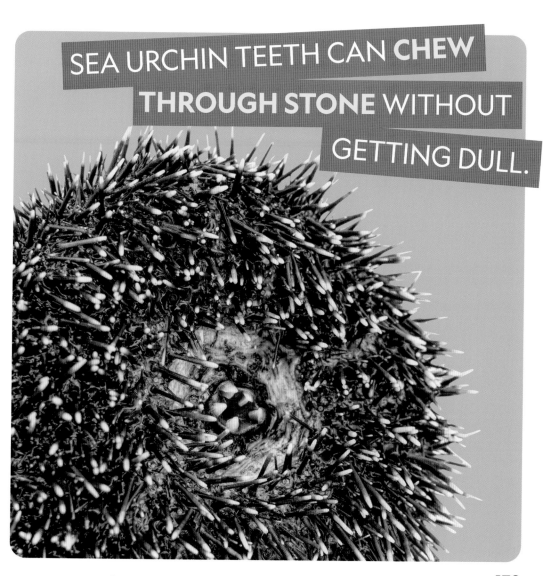

SEA URCHIN TEETH CAN **CHEW THROUGH STONE** WITHOUT GETTING DULL.

Peacock flounder can change color to match their surroundings within seconds.

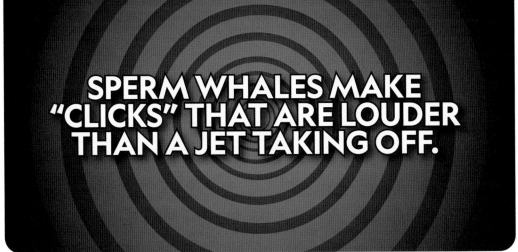

SPERM WHALES MAKE "CLICKS" THAT ARE LOUDER THAN A JET TAKING OFF.

A frilled shark has **300 TEETH.**

Frilled sharks have been swimming in the ocean since the time of the **DINOSAURS.**

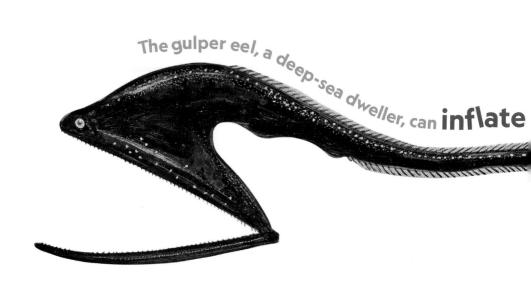

The gulper eel, a deep-sea dweller, can **inflate**

Internet data travels on **THIN WIRES** strung across the ocean floor.

its mouth like a balloon to swallow larger prey.

There are
750,000 miles (1.2 million km)
of wires—enough to
CIRCLE THE GLOBE
30 times!

WATER ERUPTING FROM VOLCANIC **DEEP-SEA VENTS** CAN REACH 750°F (400°C) — **THAT'S HOT ENOUGH TO MELT LEAD.**

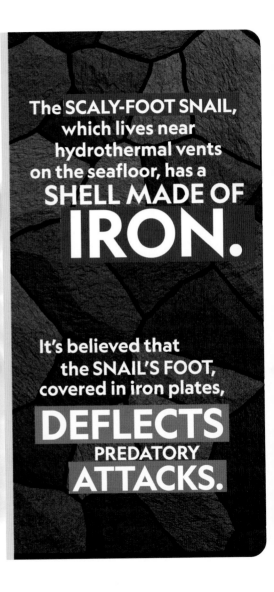

The **SCALY-FOOT SNAIL,** which lives near hydrothermal vents on the seafloor, has a **SHELL MADE OF IRON.**

It's believed that the **SNAIL'S FOOT,** covered in iron plates, **DEFLECTS** PREDATORY **ATTACKS.**

An English beach artist makes 500-foot (152-m)-wide **DRAWINGS IN SAND** and then photographs them with a **DRONE.**

AN ELEPHANT SEAL CAN **WEIGH** AS MUCH AS A **PICKUP TRUCK.**

THE STRONGEST EARTHQUAKE EVER RECORDED WAS IN THE PACIFIC OCEAN, OFF THE COAST OF SOUTHERN CHILE, IN 1960.

Trumpetfish float HEAD DOWN and SUCK UP FISH with their mouths.

DURING A 2018 OCEAN CLEANUP, MORE THAN **ONE MILLION PEOPLE** COLLECTED 97,457,984 PIECES OF TRASH.

THE SPANISH DANCER, A TYPE OF SHELL-LESS MOLLUSK, RESEMBLES A **FLAMENCO DANCER** WHEN IT SWIMS.

185

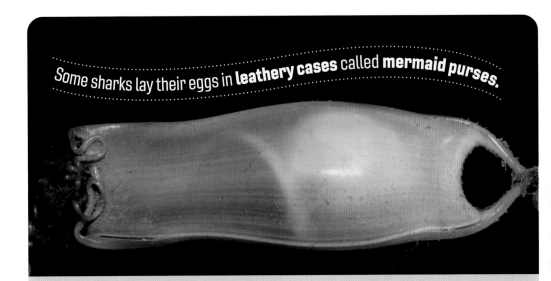

Some sharks lay their eggs in **leathery cases** called **mermaid purses.**

A female Atlantic herring can produce

200,000

eggs at one time.

One bottlenose dolphin mother **cared for an orphaned** melon-headed whale calf for three years.

SOME 2,000 YEARS AGO, ROMAN NATURALIST PLINY THE ELDER WROTE ABOUT USING SEA URCHIN ASHES TO TREAT BALDNESS.

Newborn great white sharks are as long as a bathtub.

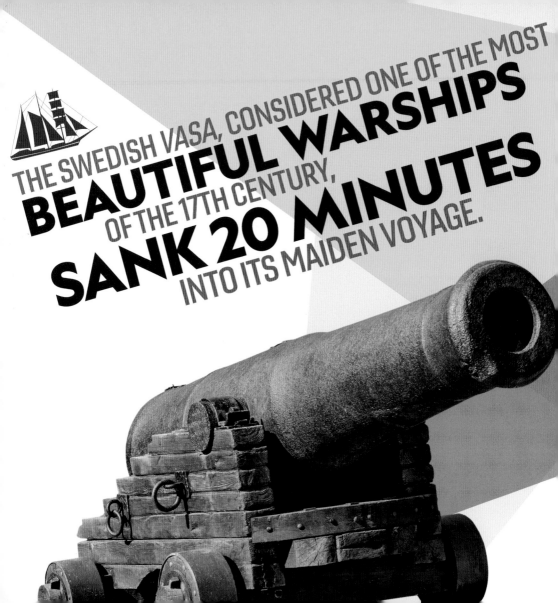

THE SHIP SANK IN PART BECAUSE THE GUN DECK WAS **OVERLOADED** WITH 64 BRONZE CANNONS.

WHEN TRAVELING AT FULL SPEED, SEAWISE GIANT, *THE MOST MASSIVE SHIP EVER BUILT, NEEDED MORE THAN FIVE MILES (8 KM) TO COME TO A STOP.*

One deep-sea octopus guarded her eggs for 4 YEARS and 5 MONTHS—the longest of any animal known.

WARNING PROTECTED BY OCTO-GUARD HOME SECURITY 24 HOUR SURVEILLANCE

(It takes one to three months for most shallow-water octopus eggs to hatch.)

Atlantic goliath groupers use their **big mouths** to **suck fish** in and swallow them whole.

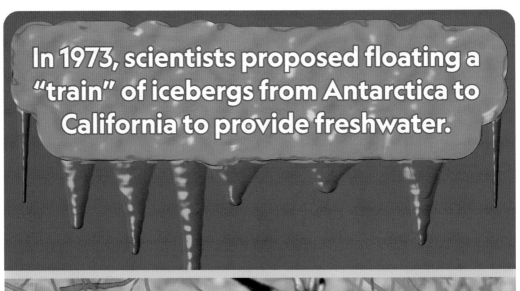

In 1973, scientists proposed floating a "train" of icebergs from Antarctica to California to provide freshwater.

Blue dragon sea slugs have **air bubbles** in their stomachs that **keep them afloat.**

Brinicles are underwater icicles that form when **frozen salt water** meets **less salty** seawater.

Antarctic icefish have **antifreeze-like proteins** in their blood so that they can **survive in subfreezing water**.

American eels travel more than 1,000 miles (1,600 km) from the Sargasso Sea in the Atlantic to freshwater lakes and rivers, where they grow into adults.

Boldface indicates illustrations.

Since 1888, the National Geographic Society has funded more than 12,000 research, exploration, and preservation projects around the world. The Society receives funds from National Geographic Partners, LLC, funded in part by your purchase. A portion of the proceeds from this book supports this vital work. To learn more, visit natgeo.com/info.

For more information, visit nationalgeographic .com, call 1-877-873-6846, or write to the following address:

National Geographic Partners
1145 17th Street N.W.
Washington, D.C. 20036-4688 U.S.A.

For librarians and teachers: nationalgeographic.com/ books/librarians-and-educators/

More for kids from National Geographic: natgeokids.com

National Geographic Kids magazine inspires children to explore their world with fun yet educational articles on animals, science, nature, and more. Using fresh storytelling and amazing photography, *Nat Geo Kids* shows kids ages 6 to 14 the fascinating truth about the world—and why they should care. **kids.nationalgeographic.com/subscribe**

For rights or permissions inquiries, please contact National Geographic Books Subsidiary Rights: bookrights@natgeo.com

Designed by Kathryn Robbins

Trade paperback ISBN: 978-1-4263-7181-3
Reinforced library binding ISBN: 978-1-4263-7182-0

The publisher would like to thank Julie Beer and Michelle Harris, authors and researchers; Grace Hill, project manager; Kathryn Williams, project editor; Hilary Andrews, photo editor; Shannon Pallatta, designer; and Anne LeongSon and Gus Tello, production assistants.

Printed in China
22/LPC/3

PHOTO CREDITS

Cover (UP LE), Eric Isselée/AS; (UP RT), wildestanimal/SS; (LO LE), Andrea Izzotti/SS; (LO RT & spine), ELENA/AS; (background), Naoki Kim/AS; 2, Eric Isselée/AS; 2-3, Naoki Kim/AS; 4-5, robertharding/AS; 6 (UP), New Africa/AS; 6 (CTR LE), tapong117/AS; 6 (CTR RT), ArteSub/Alamy Stock Photo; 6 (LO), MicroOne/SS; 7 (LE), Vittorio Bruno/AS; 7 (UP RT), AndreaTS/AS; 8 (UP), Fuad/AS; 8 (CTR), patmasari45/AS; 8 (LO), imageBROKER/AS; 9, Anton Balazh/AS; 10 (LE), Emory Kristof/NGIC; 10 (UP RT), AlexRoz/SS; 11, NatureDiver/SS; 12 (LE), mast3r/AS; 12 (RT), J. Stewart/SS; 13, Paul Souders/GI; 14-15, adamkaz/GI; 16 (UP), cloud7days/AS; 16 (LO), ohishiftl/AS; 17, Whale Research Solutions/NGIC; 18, Fisheries And Oceans Canada/AS; 19, Brent Durand/GI; 20, Superheang168/SS; 21, Carlo Pinasco/GI; 22 (LE), Michal/AS; 22 (UP RT), Alexa_Travel/SS; 22 (LO RT), Bill Varie/GI; 23, AHDesignConcepts/GI; 24-25, Viaval Tours/SS; 26 (UP), Art 27/AS; 26 (LO), dottedyeti/AS; 27, David Aguilar; 28 (UP), Eric Delmar/iStockphoto; 28 (LO LE), DM7/AS; 28 (LO CTR), Anton Starikov/SS; 28 (LO RT), sarapom/AS; 29, Christian Musat/SS; 30 (UP), Daniel/AS; 31 (UP), chocolatefather/AS; 31 (LO), Christopher Parsons/Alamy Stock Photo; 32-33, Phil Lowe/AS; 34 (UP), KK Stock/SS; 34 (LO), Sudowoodo/AS; 35, NASA/GSFC/Jeff Schmaltz/MODIS Land Rapid Response Team; 36 (UP), AP/SS; 36 (LO), David Shen/Blue Planet Archive; 37, Damsea/SS; 38-39, courtesy of Big Cedar Lodge; 40 (UP), MZPHOTO.CZ/SS; 40 (LO), Jak Wonderly/NG; 41, Robert Harding Picture Library/NGIC; 42 (LE), Designs Stock/SS; 42 (RT), ArtVille; 43, Aaron/AS; 44, tae208/GI; 45 (UP), Image Ideas; 45 (LO), W. H. Longley and Charles Martin/NGIC; 46, Todd/AS; 47 (LE), BELOW_SURFACE/GI; 47 (RT), Brian J. Skerry/NGIC; 48, Stephen Frink/Digital Vision; 49, Miyoung Han/EyeEm/AS; 50, whitcomberd/AS; 51, George Karbus Photography/GI; 52 (UP), Tarpan/SS; 52 (LO), Johan Swanepoel/SS; 53, Joost van Uffelen/SS; 54-55, 俊梁/AS; 56 (UP), enanuchit/AS; 56 (LO), prochym/AS; 57, Sabphoto/SS; 58, AFSC/NOAA/SS; 59 (UP), Paul Nicklen/NGIC; 59 (LO), Dan Thornberg/SS; 60 (UP), solarseven/SS; 60 (LO), suwatsir/AS; 61, Auscape/Universal Images Group via GI; 62-63, Per Aquum Niyama/SS; 64 (LE), Britta Pedersen/EPA/SS; 64 (LO RT), Vladislav S/SS; 65, Vlad61/SS; 66 (LE), Makc/SS; 66 (RT), Eric Isselée/SS; 67, Greg Amptman/SS; 68 (UP LE), aapsky/AS; 68 (UP CTR), CK Ma/SS; 68 (UP RT), Kletr/SS; 69, David Carbo/SS; 71 (CTR LE), Liudmyla/AS; 71 (CTR RT), UI/SS; 71 (LO), tribalium81/AS; 72, Yellow Cat/SS; 73, kondratuk/AS; 74 (LE), mrallen/AS; 74 (RT), cherylvb/AS; 75, Sabphoto/SS; 76 (LE), NOAA Okeanos Explorer Program, Gulf of Mexico 2014 Expedition; 76 (LO CTR), MisterStock/SS; 76 (LO RT), Jon Paul Dominic Cunningham/Dreamstime; 77, Tory Kallman/SS; 78, visionaryearth/AS; 79 (LE), Solent News/SS; 79 (RT), Mchudo/Dreamstime; 80 (UP), nikkytok/AS; 80 (LO), Yeti Studio/AS; 81, courtesy of the NOAA Office of Ocean Exploration and Research, Windows to the Deep 2018; 82-83, Pat/AS; 85, AlienCat/AS; 86, Rich Carey/SS; 87 (UP), Brian Lasenby/SS; 87 (LO), anemone/AS; 89 (UP), Jane Kelly/SS; 89 (LO), Paulo Oliveira/Alamy Stock Photo; 90-91, ducksmallfoto/AS; 92 (UP), Wallace Woon/EPA/SS; 92 (LO),

blumer1979/AS; 93, Frantisek Hojdysz/AS; 94, Susan Schmitz/SS; 95 (CTR), Paulo Oliveira/Alamy Stock Photo; 95, UI/SS; 96 (UP), PictureLux/The Hollywood Archive/Alamy Stock Photo; 96 (LO), Bluewater Photographer/SS; 97, courtesy of the NOAA Office of Ocean Exploration and Research; 98-99, Raymond Boyd/GI; 100, lunamarina/SS; 101, HollyHarry/SS; 102-103, viktor2013/AS; 104 (UP), SergeUWPhoto/SS; 104 (LO), Vlada Z/AS; 105, Michael Zeigler/GI; 106-107, Franco Tempesta; 108, ankudi/SS; 109 (rhino), MaZiKab/AS; 109 (goggles), photoDISC; 110 (UP), Eli Maier/SS; 110 (LO), chones/AS; 111, Matt9122/SS; 112 (UP), Stephen Frink/GI; 112 (LO), courtesy of Aquapix and Expedition to the Deep Slope 2007, NOAA-OE; 113 (LE), Gus Andi/AS; 113 (RT), Rich Carey/SS; 114-115, Tatiana Belova/AS; 116 (UP), Vladimir Wrangel/AS; 116 (LO), Vita Yarmolyuk/SS; 117, Trueog/GI; 118 (LE), iadams/AS; 118 (LO RT), Valery Evlakhov/AS; 119 (UP), Shin Okamoto/GI; 119 (LO), dzmitry/AS; 120 (UP), Ekaterina Elagina/AS; 120 (LO), helga1981/AS; 121, CampCrazy Photography/SS; 122 (UP), shanemyersphoto/AS; 122 (LO), Kletr/SS; 123, Piotr Szczap/AS; 124-125, Uryadnikov Sergey/AS; 126 (UP), Boyd Hendrikse/SS; 126 (LO), Dotted Yeti/SS; 127, Kalyakan/AS; 128 (UP), Pär Edlund/Dreamstime; 128 (LO), James Kelley/AS; 129, Neil Bromhall/SS; 130 (UP), lonlywolf/SS; 130 (LO LE), Eduardo/AS; 130 (LO RT), Jon/AS; 131, Keneva Photography/SS; 132-133, Risto Mattila; 134 (UP), oleon17/AS; 134 (LO), bekirevren/AS; 135, wildestanimal/GI; 136 (UP), Kirill Umrikhin/SS; 136 (LO), History and Art Collection/Alamy Stock Photo; 137, Vladimir Wrangel/AS; 138, SuslO/SS; 138-139, dottedyeti/AS; 139, Aleksandar Nakovski/AS; 140, KYTan/SS; 141, Subphoto/AS; 142-143 (UP), memej/SS; 142-143 (LO), Chase Dekker/SS; 144 (UP), Blaine Harrington III/Alamy Stock Photo; 144 (LO RT), Andrey_Kuzmin/SS; 145, Guo Zihao/EyeEm/GI; 146-147, Ken Kiefer/Cultura Creative/Alamy Stock Photo; 148 (UP), jaroslava V/SS; 148 (LO), Christopher Ewing/Dreamstime; 149 (LE), Arctium Lappa/SS; 149 (RT), pclark2/AS; 149 (wig), easyasaofficial/AS; 149 (pearls), byjeng/AS; 150 (UP), Michael/AS; 150 (LO), Hotshotsworldwide/Dreamstime; 151, Clemens Vanderwerf/AS; 153, Alex Mustard/Nature Picture Library; 154-155, Al Giddings/NGIC; 156-157 (UP), Sait Ozgur Gedikoglu/SS; 156-157 (LO), Save Jungle/AS; 158, GeraldRobertFischer/AS; 159, veliferum/AS; 160 (UP), BillionPhotos.com/AS; 160 (LO), Soranome/SS; 161, Gary Florin/SS; 162-163, Anna segeren/SS; 164 (UP), Olga Khoroshunova/AS; 164 (LO), Brian J. Skerry/NGIC; 165, Mats/AS; 166 (CTR), Miroslav Stimac/SS; 166 (RT), Fer Gregory/SS; 167 (UP), aleksangel/AS; 167 (CTR), Jennifer White Maxwell/SS; 167 (LO), Ethan Daniels/SS; 168-169, orifec_a31/SS; 171, Drew/AS; 172 (UP), vadidak/AS; 172 (LO), yeshaya/AS; 173, EKH-Pictures/AS; 174, Monty Chandler/AS; 175, SS; 176-177 (UP), Encyclopaedia Britannica/Uig/SS; 176-177 (LO), Andrey_Kuzmin/SS; 179, Stephen Frink/GI; 180-181, Mike Newman/Solent News/SS; 182 (LE), L Barnwell/SS; 182 (CTR), AWesleyFloyd/SS; 182 (RT), EvgeniiAnd/AS; 183, whitcomberd/AS; 184, Andrea Izzotti/AS; 185 (LE), photka/SS; 185 (RT), Dai Mar Tamarack/SS; 186, Tim Wijgerde/SS; 187, Janos Rautonen/SS; 188, martin/AS; 189, frantisek hojdysz/AS; 190 (UP), Yevheniia Lytvynovych/SS; 190 (LO), vadim_orlov/AS; 191, Martin Bergsma/SS; 192 (LO LE), Vectorovich/AS; 192 (LO RT), alexmillos/SS; 193, Janos/AS; 194 (LO), Sahara Frost/AS; 195, Jason Edwards/NGIC; 196, Khing Pinta/SS; 197, vadiml/AS

GO DEEPER!

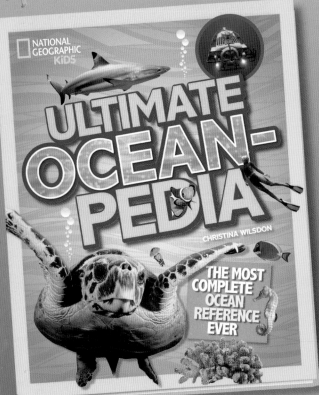

Intrigued by the Weird But True! facts you've just read? Dive into *Ultimate Oceanpedia* for more info. It's swimming with fascinating facts, photos, and stories about our amazing ocean and the sea life within it.